W9-BGZ-005

THE KIDS' LIBRARY OF MARTIAL ARTS™

JUDO

Pamela Randall

The Rosen Publishing Group's

New York

Published in 1999 by The Rosen Publishing Group, Inc.
29 East 21st Street, New York, NY 10010

First Edition

Book Design: Danielle Primiceri

Photo Illustrations by Seth Dinnerman

Randall, Pamela.
    Judo / by Pamela Randall.
        p.   cm. — (Martial arts)
    Includes index.
    Summary: Introduces the history, basic moves, and terminology of this martial art.
    ISBN 0-8239-5238-X
    1. Judo—Juvenile literature. [1. Judo.] I. Title.
    II. Series: Randall, Pamela. Martial arts.
  GV1114.R38 1998
  796.815'2—dc21   97-49270
                                                                    CIP
                                                                    AC

Manufactured in the United States of America

Contents

Kyle and His Dad

Kyle's dad was on his college wrestling team. Kyle wants to be just like his dad when he grows up. "When I go to college, I'm going to be a wrestler too," Kyle said.

"You don't have to wait until college to play sports," Kyle's dad said. "How would you like to learn judo? You could take lessons with your friend Dalia."

Kyle was happy when his dad signed him up for lessons in the **martial art** (MAR-shul ART) called judo.

Judo School

The students in Kyle's class all practice on large mats. In some schools, the mats are made of straw. This is how they were made in the past. In other schools, like Kyle's, they're made of foam.

Kyle, Dalia, and their classmates take their classes barefoot. They wear special uniforms. This uniform is called a *judogi* (JOO-doh-gee). The *judogi* has large, baggy pants called **zubon** (ZOO-bohn), and a baggy jacket with floppy sleeves called a **sode** (SOH-day).

Wearing a judogi lets students stretch and practice their moves more easily than in street clothes. ▶

Kyle's White Belt

Kyle's uniform also has a belt. The belt is called an **obi** (OH-bee). Kyle's *obi* is white, because he is a beginner. Dalia's *obi* is yellow. She is more advanced than Kyle. In time Kyle will advance too, and the color of his belt will keep changing as he learns more. Kyle and Dalia hope to have black belts one day. Black belts are given only to judo students of the highest rank, or skill level.

◀ *As students advance in judo, they earn different colored belts. These belts let people know what their ranks are.*

A Little Judo History

Judo is based on a martial art called ju jitsu. Ju jitsu is also called ju jutsu. It was created in the 1700s. The modern form of judo practiced today was started by a Japanese man named Jigaro Kano. In 1882 he opened a **dojo** (DOH-joh), or a school for judo, in Tokyo, Japan.

In 1889 Jigaro Kano gave a judo **demonstration** (deh-mun-STRAY-shun) in France. People liked what they saw and became interested in learning judo. Soon judo spread to other countries.

Many of the martial arts, such as ju jitsu, ▶
were created in Japan.

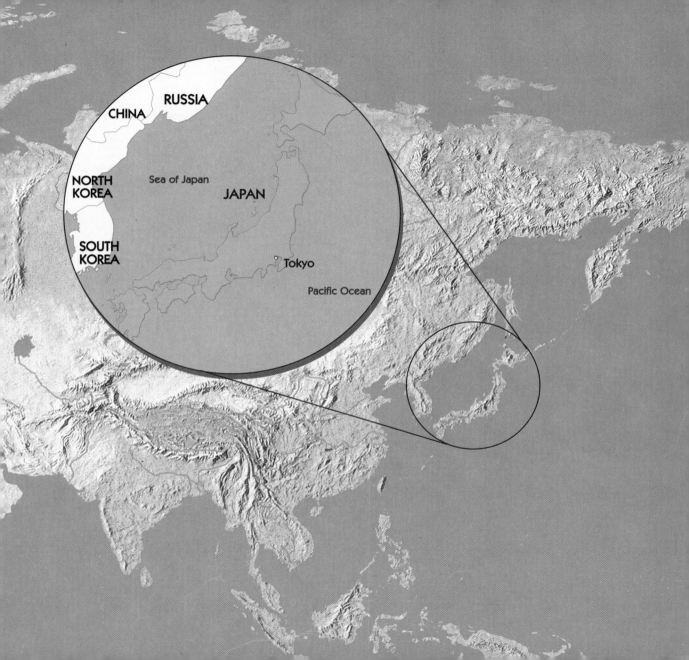

RUSSIA

CHINA

NORTH
KOREA

Sea of Japan

JAPAN

SOUTH
KOREA

Tokyo

Pacific Ocean

The Body and the Mind

In the past people used judo **defensively** (dih-FEN-siv-lee). But today judo is used in **competition** (KOM-peh-TIH-shun). Judo students may also **spar** (SPAR) with each other during class.

Gentleness was very important to Jigaro Kano when he started judo. Sadly, few dojos teach this part of judo anymore. But, like most other martial arts, judo involves mental strength as well as physical strength. So most judo **instructors** (in-STRUK-terz) still teach students that it's important to be calm when doing judo.

Being calm and relaxed helps judo students perform their moves better.

Falling

The first thing Kyle learned in his judo lessons was how to fall the right way. It's important to be able to fall without getting hurt. Kyle and Dalia stand facing each other. Using what they've learned in class, they try to throw each other onto the mat.

Kyle stays on his feet. When Kyle finally throws Dalia onto the mat, she is okay. The teacher taught them how to fall without getting hurt.

Kyle helps Dalia up. Then they will spar again.

Escape!

Kyle has also learned how to escape when Dalia gets him in a hold. Since Kyle and Dalia aren't **competing** (kum-PEE-ting) with each other, they help each other learn.

First, Dalia and Kyle bow to each other. Then they try to use their judo moves on each other. The teacher watches to see who has learned well and who needs more practice. But Dalia isn't trying to do better than Kyle. She just wants to do better than she did last week.

Like Dalia and Kyle, these students are learning to use judo to free themselves when an opponent has them in a headlock.

Stronger Bodies

When Kyle came to the dojo for his first lesson, the teacher had the class do push-ups. Kyle was **disappointed** (dih-suh-POYN-ted). "We do that in gym class!" he said. Kyle wanted to learn judo moves right away. Dalia helped explain that exercise is a big part of judo.

Kyle realized that these push-ups aren't always the same as the ones he does in gym. Some are done with open palms. Others are done with closed fists.

Judo students practice stretching exercises such as this one to get in shape. ▶

One in the Middle

Kyle and Dalia's class plays games that teach them judo skills. In a game called One in the Middle, a student is blindfolded and put in the middle of a circle.

The other students try to sneak past her. The blindfolded student tries to catch one of the others and get him in a judo hold. If she does, she can take off the blindfold and put it on the student that she pinned.

Kids learn many things in judo class and they work very hard. But they also have a lot of fun!

A Prize for Kyle

After Kyle studies judo for a few months, a competition is held. Students of the same rank, or belt color, and who weigh about the same, spar with each other. Competitions let the instructor see how much each student has learned. Dalia won her competition. Even though he didn't win, Kyle advanced to a different color belt.

A few months later, Dalia and Kyle entered another competition. This time they both won prizes! Dalia and Kyle are proud of how much they have learned.

Glossary

compete (kum-PEET) Trying hard to win something.

competition (kom-peh-TIH-shun) A contest.

defensively (dih-FEN-siv-lee) Guarding against an attack or a fight.

demonstration (deh-mun-STRAY-shun) Showing people how to do something by acting it out.

disappointed (dih-suh-POYN-ted) Feeling let down.

dojo (DOH-joh) A school where judo is taught and practiced.

instructor (in-STRUK-ter) A person who teaches.

judogi (JOO-doh-gee) The uniform worn when practicing judo.

martial art (MAR-shul ART) Any of the arts of self-defense or fighting that is practiced as a sport.

obi (OH-bee) A belt that shows a student's rank.

spar (SPAR) To have a practice fight.

sode (SOH-day) A baggy jacket with floppy sleeves that is worn for judo.

zubon (ZOO-bohn) The large, baggy pants worn for judo.

Index